101 Ways To Save MONEY And ENERGY In Your GROCERY STORE

By David A. Troesh
LEED AP

In cooperation with
Aztec Energy Partners

INFINITY
PUBLISHING

ISBN 0-7414-5712-1

Extra copies of this book can be purchased from
www.DaveTroesh.com

Published by:

INFINITY PUBLISHING

INFINITY PUBLISHING
1094 New DeHaven Street, Suite 100
West Conshohocken, PA 19428-2713
Info@buybooksontheweb.com
www.buybooksontheweb.com
Toll-free (877) BUY BOOK
Local Phone (610) 941-9999
Fax (610) 941-9959

Printed in the United States of America

Published January 2011

PREFACE

We know you are too busy to read this book, so we made it short, non-technical and easy to read. Whether you manage a gas station mini-mart or a 100,000-square-foot big box market, you have a thousand things to check on or do with neither time enough nor help enough to do them. Beyond all the problems you face every day just trying to make a profit, now there is pressure from every side to save energy and go green. This book helps you to either just scratch the surface of sustainability or dive as deep as you want into ways to save money while greening your store. There are far too many things to do yourself so, as you skim the three lists, think about creating a Green Team.

Grocery stores consume more electricity and gas than any other industry in the commercial sector. Compared to most businesses, reducing our energy consumption is easy and can actually save you money. **According to the EPA, every energy dollar saved translates into $59.00 of groceries that you don't have to sell in order to make the same profit.**

Each of the three chapters starts with a simple checklist followed by a more in-depth description of each money-saving upgrade.

Chapter One describes fifty ways to improve your bottom line virtually for free.

Chapter Two suggests a few dozen other ways to spend only a little money to watch your energy costs plummet while your profits rise.

If you are looking to invest in your company's future and wonder about the best ways to save more money and be significantly more profitable while going seriously green, go to Chapter Three. There we show you what both major and minor grocery chains all over the country are doing to improve their profitability, sustainability and simply stay alive in one of the most competitive industries imaginable.

See the appendices for: A) A Store Green Team Preventative Maintenance Checklist B) Energy Related Terms and Definitions C) Energy Facts D) On-line Resources E) Vendor Preventative Maintenance Checklist F) Employee Energy Survey.

It makes no difference whether you manage a 1000 or a 100,000 square-foot store. If you sell groceries, your energy problems are essentially the same. To save you the research time, the suggestions here were gathered from dozens of up-to-date sources and apply to virtually any food retailer with refrigeration, lights and an A/C unit. That's just about all of us!

Note: Depending on the size of your store, some of the listed upgrades don't apply. Adapt the lists to your specific needs to save the most money and energy.

These materials are meant to examine typical operations and technologies. They are meant to clarify and illustrate typical situations and must be appropriately adapted to individual circumstances. Moreover, the materials are not intended to provide legal advice or establish legal standards of reasonable behavior.

CHAPTER ONE

Fifty Free or Nearly-Free Upgrades

As you will see, nearly all of this chapter's upgrades necessitate only a slight shift in your store team's environmental philosophy and/or a little more attention to detail. None of these are difficult and, cumulatively, they all have an immediate and measurable bottom line payback.

Some of the tasks listed below are obvious. Hopefully, many of them are already part of an established sustainability program. You probably thought about some of the others but never realized how much money they can save your store. First, check off what you have already accomplished on the following list. Next, see the short explanations and simple suggestions about how best to attack the uncompleted part of your Chapter One list.

Easy Savings Checklist

LIGHTING

- o Replace incandescent lamps with CFLs (compact fluorescent lamps).
- o Turn off unneeded sales floor, accent and department lighting.
- o Reduce lighting by removing selected sales floor lamps.
- o Do not over light.

- Remove excess lighting in stockroom and storage spaces.
- Take advantage of existing natural daylight to lower interior lighting.
- Minimize exterior illuminated sign usage.
- Turn off parking lot lights during the day and after your last employee goes home.
- Adjust timers to accommodate the seasons, daylight savings and changing store hours.
- Pursue rebates on all unplanned capital purchases and/or repairs.
- Take advantage of your utility company's "Time Related Demand Metering" rules.
- Dissect your electric bill.

HVAC

- Set your cold thermostat at 78° and hot at 68° degrees.
- Seal off unused offices or rarely used areas especially the machine and electrical rooms.
- Close exterior doors.
- Turn off exhaust fans when not in use.
- Turn heater pilot lights and timers off in summer.
- Keep air grills and registers clean and unblocked.
- Lower water heater temperature to legal minimum.

REFRIGERATION

- Use correct temperatures. Colder isn't always better.

- Create accountability for case temperatures.
- Create an Employee Preventative Maintenance Schedule.
- Properly load refrigerated equipment.
- Close walk-in freezer and cooler doors.
- Keep refrigerators four inches from the wall.
- Clean self-contained refrigerator coils regularly.
- Clean cooler drains, drain pans and honeycombs regularly.
- Anticipate Health Department issues.

OFFICE EQUIPMENT AND STORE OPERATIONS

- Create a Green Team.
- Unplug charger units when not in use.
- Use power strips dedicated to specific equipment.
- Activate power management software on your computer.
- Print on both sides of all memos.
- Use recycled paper.
- Recycle more than just paper.

COOKING

- Stagger equipment turn-on times and selectively preheat ovens and grills.
- Turn down fryers between batches.
- Shut off exhaust hoods when not in use.
- Recalibrate broilers and ovens.

- o Restrict warmer usage.
- o Cook during off-peak hours.
- o Cook in large quantities.
- o Remove excess ice and water before frying.
- o Load and unload ovens quickly.
- o Use flat-bottom pans with lids.
- o Microwave ovens are energy savers. Use them first.
- o Put timers on coffee makers.
- o Direct cooling fans toward employees.
- o Polish heat reflectors.
- o Clean burners regularly.

Checklist Suggestions and Tips

LIGHTING

Replace incandescent lamps with CFLs (compact fluorescent lamps). Replace incandescent light bulbs with compact fluorescent lamps as they wear out. The CFLs cost a little more but last at least ten times longer. Different types are available to fit almost any application and many come with rebates. Make sure you get the proper lamp to take full advantage of the reflective capacity of your existing light fixture (i.e. screw-in CFL flood lamps instead of the pigtail variety where needed). Changing out the lamps with the longest daily burn time will net you the fastest payback. Based on a $.15 /kWh rate, selectively replacing only twenty 60 watt spotlights with 24 watt CFL spotlights will save you about $700/year. Caution: There are dozens of really cheap CFLs available on the market today. They don't last. To get the expected long life, buy only Energy Star® rated lamps.

The chart below shows the possible savings when replacing incandescent lamps with quality CFLs with a comparable light output.

INCANDESCENT vs. CFL SAVINGS

INCANDESCENT		CFLs		
Watts	Average Anticipated Life	Watts	Average Anticipated Life	Potential Annual Savings
40	1500 hours	7	10,000	47.17
60	1000	13	10,000	63.45
75	750	18	10,000	79.08
100	750	26	10,000	102.67

The savings shown above are based on the differences in lamp life at $.15 / kWh.

Turn off unneeded sales floor, accent and department lighting. Turn off half your sales floor lighting fifteen minutes after closing and leave them off until fifteen minutes before opening the next morning. Turn off all case, track and accent lighting at closing time. Turn off service department lighting as early as possible.

Reduce lighting by removing selected sales floor lamps. A number of stores have accomplished measurably successful energy reduction by simply removing one or more lamps from dual or multi-lamp fixtures (i.e. half the lamps from a dual or four-lamp trough ceiling fixture). Actually, you save two ways when you reduce your ceiling lamp count. First, and most obvious, using only half of your lamps burns only about half as much electricity. (There is still a small amount of electricity running through your unused ballast.) Second, your A/C only needs to compensate for half as much lamp-generated heat as before. Tip: It is not surprising that over 20% of your electrical usage cost is for lighting when you consider that removing just one typical T-8, 32 watt fluorescent lamp can save you over $30/year.

Do not over light. Too much light is worse on your eyes than too little. Just because a light fixture can accommodate more lamps is no reason to install them. Based on a $.15 /kWh rate, reducing your lighting by just 1000 watts for twenty hours every week will reduce your electric bill by nearly $150. Most stores can accomplish these savings by simply adjusting the on/off times on their cold case lights and accent lighting. In the photo below, the combination of track lighting, hanging fluorescent lighting and lots of windows is a great example of overlighting.

Figure 1. Extreme overlighting. Photo by Hussmann Refrigeration. Reprinted with permission. All rights reserved.

Remove excess lighting in stockroom and storage spaces. Remove any extra lamps in seldom-used rooms (i.e. janitor closets, computer dark rooms and mezzanine fixture storage areas). There is a smaller potential for savings here, but even reducing consumption by 1000 kWh can net you a $150 annual savings. Tip: Don't create an unsafe condition or remove any emergency lighting.

Take advantage of existing natural daylight to lower interior lighting. Adjust your sales floor lighting during that short time everyday when the sun is shining most brilliantly through your front windows. If your store is blessed with skylights, make sure that your photo sensors are operating properly and that your EMS system is lowering your light levels as far as reasonable. In a store with east-facing windows, taking advantage of the morning sun by turning off a couple rows of lights can also net you a big return. Note: A recent study showed that 90% of the population doesn't notice a 10% reduction in light levels. (lumens)

Minimize exterior illuminated sign usage. Make sure your exterior signage doesn't stay on all night or even worse, burn all day when no one can tell the difference. If you are paying for space and a percentage of the electric bill on a lighted pylon sign as part of your CAM (common area maintenance), make sure your signs only stay illuminated when appropriate and that you are being charged the correct amount as stated in your lease agreement.

Turn off parking lot lights during the day and after your last employee goes home. Reduce parking lot lighting to a bare, but safe minimum after the last employee exits the lot. Make this circuit easy to override to keep your employees safe if they stay longer than usual.

Adjust timers to accommodate the seasons, daylight savings and changing store hours. Thousands of dollars are wasted each year with the faulty justification that "just an hour doesn't make any difference." Check and adjust timers monthly to match the changing sunrise and sunset times and if you have varying opening and closing times.

Pursue rebates on all unplanned capital purchases and/or repairs. In California, where this book was written, there are a number of creative programs designed to recoup your energy investment dollars. Call your local utility company or check its website to see if any of your upcoming capital expenses or emergency repairs can be covered by rebates. Oddly enough, many utilities will actually reward you with cash for buying less of their product. You will be surprised how readily available this money can be. It is worth a quick call to find out how you can qualify.

Take advantage of your utility company's "Time Related Demand Metering" rules. Many electric utility companies impose a "Demand Time" billing charge on their high-usage customers. Your monthly demand charge can be based on your highest electrical usage during any single fifteen minute incremental time period. For example, if you come in early and quickly turn on all your lights, ovens, appliances and the air conditioning, the electricity you used to power up everything at once sets your demand rate for the month. You can easily lower your demand time rate by staggering your appliance and lighting turn-on times over one or two hours and never illuminating 100% of your lights until just before your store opens.

Dissect your Electric bill. There are several rate programs that can save you money. You might very well be stuck on the most costly plan simply because somebody checked the wrong box on your utility start-up form when you first opened. Unlike regular retailers, your energy provider is glad to help you reduce the amount of money you pay them every month. They even have teams of well-trained customer service specialists to help you find ways to lower your energy related operating costs.

HVAC

Set your cold thermostat at 78° and hot at 68° degrees. Before you set your thermostats, make sure they are accurate, then lock them to help keep them accurate. Even without interference from your store team, most will drift several degrees every year. Calibrating and adjusting your thermostats has an instant payback. That accomplished, next adjust your A/C timers or EMS to take advantage of slow times. Don't preheat (or pre-cool) your store before opening. Wait until you have been open a while (perhaps an hour or so). Same at closing time. If you don't have EMS controls, shut down your A/C an hour before closing or as early as the outside temperature allows it. Tip: When cooling, raising the set temperature 1° saves 2% of your A/C costs. When heating, lowering your temperature set point will save you up to 3%. A final note: Small area temperatures (i.e. an office area) should be adjusted by altering the airflow through that specific air register, not by adjusting the entire system.

Seal off unused offices and rarely used areas especially the machine and electrical rooms. If an area is only occasionally visited, it does not require ongoing conditioning. Close vents and all doors to untrafficked areas. The most obvious are mezzanine and/or secure storage areas, janitor closets and private offices.

Close exterior doors. Don't heat or cool the great outdoors. A poorly operating automatic front door can cost thousands every year in wasted A/C or heating, far more than the cost of repair. Don't leave your front doors open in the vain hope that your customers will feel more welcome. Pay particular attention to the receiving doors. Keep them sealed against the weather and closed when not in use.

Turn off exhaust fans when not in use. Hoods are designed to suck out smoke, steam, cooking smells and the occasional gusts of hot air from your ovens, chicken fryers and other appliances. While your hood is fulfilling its primary function, it is also sucking out your expensively conditioned air. Shut down all hoods and department exhaust fans when not in use. Tip: You can save over $100 per year for every extra hour per day that an 8' hood is shut off.

Turn heater pilot lights and timers off in summer. If you are uncomfortable with the technology, the gas company will help you deactivate your heater pilot lights. Newer models have electronically activated pilot lights that don't need your attention. The heating system should be deactivated except when definitely needed to combat the cold.

Keep air grills and registers clean and unblocked. Remove the clutter around all grills, registers and diffusers. Increasing the potential airflow reduces the run time on your A/C motors and extends their life. Many stores compromise their A/C efficiency by accidentally blocking air intakes in the back room or on the mezzanine level with fixtures and store supplies.

Lower water heater temperature to legal minimum.. Your hot water heater should be set to generate hot water only as hot as the health department mandates (usually 120° to 140°). Setting the temperature higher is both wasteful and dangerous.

REFRIGERATION

Use correct temperatures. Colder isn't always better. Closely follow these industry temperature standard ranges for each type of case. The recommended standards are:

Dairy = 32 to 36°	Frozen Food = 0 to -5°
Meat = 28 to 30°	Ice Cream = -8 to -12°
Meat/deli = 32 to 36°	Produce = 35 to 40°

Create accountability for case temperatures. You and your store team already walk your cases to check temperatures a number of times each day. Make sure everyone knows how to recognize a real problem. Post defrost times on each case to save expensive wasted calls to your refrigeration contractor.

Create an Employee Preventative Maintenance Schedule. Include at a minimum the following tasks: cleaning your ice machines, cleaning the window track on your service cases, cleaning the honeycombs on all the cases, cleaning case lights and reflectors, removing dirt and debris around fan motors and properly stocking merchandise within your cold case air curtains. Please see Appendix A for a more complete Sample Employee Preventative Maintenance Checklist.

Properly load refrigerated equipment. Pay close attention to the load lines on your cases. There are critical airflows across and around both the front and back of cold case and freezer shelves that must be kept clear for proper and efficient air circulation. On an open-front cold case or island, exceeding the load limits diverts the air curtain flow away from your case and into the store. Both your heating and refrigeration costs increase because using your refrigeration system to help cool your store costs 40% more than properly using your A/C.

Close walk-in freezer and cooler doors. This is one of the easiest money savers. Keeping the freezer and cooler doors closed tight when no one is inside can save you over $2000/year. Train your team to keep them shut. Hang a sign with a big dollar sign on each door as a reminder. Tip: Moisture from the air will freeze on the unheated portions of the door and frame. If not periodically removed, the ice build-up will block the door from closing and knock the doorframe out of plumb, which is expensive to repair.

Figure 2. Sample freezer door sign. Photograph courtesy of SUPERVALU INC. © 2009. All rights reserved. Reprinted with permission.

Keep refrigerators four inches from the wall. Refrigerator coils need moving air flowing around them to operate properly. Don't set your self-contained refrigerators or freezers tight against the wall where they can't breathe.

Clean self-contained refrigerator coils regularly. Keep your self-contained refrigerator coils clean, including the break-room refrigerator. An occasional vacuuming will significantly extend the machine's life by decreasing the motor run time. Plus: Keeping coils clean can reduce energy consumption by 25%. If you have a self-contained ice case or floral cooler, remember to vacuum the accumulated dust from those coils, too.

Clean cooler drains, drain pans and honeycombs regularly. Since drains and drain pans are out of site they are typically ignored until they clog up and trigger an expensive repair problem. Clogged honeycombs are more of an energy issue because the refrigeration equipment has to work harder to keep your cases cold. Depending on your store, once or twice a year should be enough.

Anticipate Health Department issues. The following are a few cleanliness "Hot Button" issues with many Health Department inspectors. Accomplishing these tasks will lower both your refrigeration costs and hopefully, your stress level during an inspection.

- Continual daily cleaning of all hinges, handles and gaskets on cold cases displaying open food or meat.
- Continual daily cleaning of all cold case sliding door tracks.
- Periodic flushing and cleaning of the slimy yeast-based residue from inside the ice machine.
- Store your ice scoop outside the ice machine.
- Periodically clean all dairy and freezer door gaskets.

OFFICE EQUIPMENT AND STORE OPERATIONS

Create a Green Team. There are closet environmentalists in all walks of life. Give all your employees the "Energy Survey for Employees" in Appendix F to find the most fervent ones in your store. Task them to work on the Chapter One upgrades then monitor the store's progress. Share the changes in your electric bill as their work comes to fruition. Topics for your "Green Team" to address include: maintenance, warranties, operational schedules, set points, equipment start-up/shutdown, emergency procedures, air quality, ambient temperatures, adopt-a-door, recycling, lighting and new employee energy-consciousness training. See the www. awarenessideas.com website to learn more ways to keep your team involved and enthused. An inspired Green Team working on this list can save you a fortune.

Unplug charger units when not in use. Charger units for phones, hand-held scanners and belt printers draw nearly as much electricity when charging as when on standby. Keep the chargers unplugged unless actually in use. Tip: Power strips are perfect for this application as long as everyone remembers to click the 'on' switch when they plug back in their equipment.

Use power strips dedicated to specific equipment. Many types of office equipment, especially printers and monitors suck phantom electricity even when not in use. Centralize these when possible to run off a power strip to simplify turning them all off at once. A combined computer and CRT burn close to 150 watts of power. Turning them off for only eight hours every night will save $65.00 per year. If you have to leave the computer on as part of a system, at least power down the monitor and printer overnight.

Activate power management software on your computer. If your computer doesn't have a power management system, you can download free software from Energy Star®. (www.energystar.gov/benchmark - ENERGY STAR'S® power management software). Properly used, a good power management system can reduce your computer system power usage by up to 90%.

Print on both sides of all memos. Draw a quick yellow highlighter stripe across unneeded (and unwrinkled) memos, then feed them back into your printer's paper tray. It is a very small thing that makes a very strong statement to your employees about your commitment to the environment. Besides, every tree saved from the paper mill reduces carbon dioxide emissions, air pollution and is an eco-victory you can share with your employees.

Use recycled paper. Unless you are printing a document going out to a special customer, use paper with a high-recycled content. Use the least expensive paper available for in-store written communications.

Recycle more than just paper. The grocery industry generates millions of tons of hard and soft plastic and of course, cardboard. As industry finds more uses for recycled material, the task of recycling becomes both easier and often a potential income stream. Call local recyclers to find ways to efficiently and inexpensively recycle as much store-generated trash as possible. Tip: Most stores generate so few cans and plastic bottles that they simply donate them to a worthy cause or use the proceeds to fund a store party.

COOKING

Stagger equipment turn-on times and selectively preheat ovens and grills. Rarely are oven and chicken fryer warm-up times over twenty minutes (usually under ten minutes). Research your equipment's preheat times so that you never turn them on earlier than needed. (Post the warm-up times on the unit.) Instruct your bakery and deli teams never to automatically turn on their equipment when they first walk into the department. Instead, challenge them to coordinate the turn-on time, warm-up time and start-of-cooking time to use as little energy as possible.

Turn down fryers between batches. Unless you are immediately cooking another batch, reset your fryer to a stand-by temperature as soon as you pull out the basket. Post a small (water and grease-proof) sign near the fryers showing stand-by temperatures and preheat times. Tip: When you lower your fryer to a standby temperature of around 200°, it typically only takes about two minutes to get it back up to full temperature.

Shut off exhaust hoods when not in use. Turning off the exhaust, make-up air and lights on your 8' hood for an extra hour each day can save you about $200/ year.

Recalibrate broilers and ovens. Make sure that your broilers and ovens are calibrated correctly. Cooking a few degrees hotter than recommended not only wastes energy but also effects both product texture and taste. Oven door gaskets wear with age which can alter cooking temperatures. Your bakery products will cook more evenly and you will save energy by keeping your oven doors in good repair. The ROI is short, so it's smart not to postpone the maintenance call.

Restrict warmer usage. Hot cases are another major piece of equipment that typically gets turned-on far too early. Most chicken warmers typically come up to proper holding temperature in about 20 to 30 minutes. Coordinate the turn-on with the need. Being too prepared, too early is a costly waste of energy.

Cook during off-peak hours. The demand for electricity is highest in the afternoon between noon and 6:00 p.m., so naturally the "Premium Peak Period" energy cost is highest then, too. Many stores have arranged special significantly reduced utility rates by using on-demand programs. In exchange for an overall lower rate, the stores agree to manually or automatically reduce their electrical consumption by shutting down certain equipment (usually an A/C unit) for a pre-determined amount of time. Talk to your utility representative to see if they have an acceptable plan that fits your store.

Cook in large quantities. The labor and energy involved in cooking a fryer full of chicken is almost exactly the same as cooking only half that much. If you can sell it, cook it.

Remove excess ice and water before frying. Extra ice and/or water on fried foods will only have a minimal effect on the taste and texture. However, it will cause splattering and lower the temperature of your cooking oil causing your fryer to work harder and use more electricity.

Load and unload ovens quickly. Don't leave your oven doors open any longer than absolutely necessary. You already spent money preheating your oven, quickly closing the door retains the warm air to use again.

Use flat-bottom pans with lids. Flat bottom pans provide a larger surface area to make the most efficient use of your heat source. A lid contains the heat inside your pot where it belongs rather than escaping into your cooking area where it can raise your A/C cost.

Microwave ovens are energy savers. Use them first. Your microwave oven is one of the highest efficiency appliances in your prep area or kitchen. Ranked by energy usage, next come ovens, steamers then fryers. The worst energy burners are griddles and broilers.

Put timers on coffee makers. If your coffee maker isn't already equipped with an automatic timer, plug it into one. An ignored coffee pot will boil its contents down to powder, smell horribly and crack the carafe. Even if it doesn't break, it's so labor intensive to clean, you are better off throwing it away.

Direct cooling fans toward employees. The use of directional fans is an inexpensive way to help cool a food prep area rather than waiting for the A/C to catch up. Studies show that, even though the change isn't real, people perceive a 5° temperature drop as soon as the moving air hits them. Make sure the refreshing air is blowing toward your employees, not the food.

Polish heat reflectors. Take advantage of the physics behind heat reflectivity by cleaning all the reflective surfaces inside your ovens and broilers.

Clean burners regularly. Clogged burner ports cause uneven heat distribution and waste gas by extending cooking times.

CHAPTER TWO

Low Cost Savings

Most of the upgrades described here in Chapter Two can be accomplished at a minimal cost. A conversation with both your refrigeration and A/C contractors will help you chose which of their upgrades will have the fastest potential paybacks. For some of the tasks, you simply have to wait until something breaks and then replace it with energy-efficient equipment. Others, you can do yourself, even if you are not mechanically inclined.

Review and prioritize the list below. We realize that some of these corrections seem like pipe dreams, but others you can start today. Remember, a lot of the paybacks on these energy-saving improvements are less than a year, so do what you can now to improve your bottom line.

Easy Savings Checklist

LIGHTING

- Start with replacing just five barely burning incandescent lamps with CFLs.
- Clean light fixtures and lamps.
- Install exterior timers.
- Replace mercury vapor lights.
- Install occupancy sensors in all closed rooms.

- Replace neon and accent lighting with LED (Light Emitting Diode) lamps.
- Install 'second generation' T-8 lamps.
- Replace yellow or hazy lenses, diffusers and globes.
- Buy only Energy Star® rated lamps.

HVAC

- Install timers to shut down non-essential systems during off hours.
- Set economizers properly.
- Create and carefully follow a preventative maintenance schedule.
- Pretreat cooling tower water.
- Remove scale from heat exchange units.
- Replace worn or cracked weather stripping and seal up all holes.
- Install reflective tint on windows.
- Use portable space heaters or fans in enclosed rooms.
- Seal and insulate A/C ducts in unconditioned areas.
- Install ceiling fans in receiving.
- Install door sweeps on exterior doors.

REFRIGERATION

- Adjust defrost controls.
- Carefully follow your Refrigeration System Preventative Maintenance schedule.
- Perform a dollar bill test on all freezer and cooler doors. (It shouldn't slip out!)

- Service walk-in boxes annually.
- Install anti-sweat heater controls on frozen food doors.
- Install insulation on bare refrigeration lines.
- Install swinging doors to cooling areas.
- Replace T-12 case lighting with T-8 lamps or LED lighting.
- Install automatic door closers on walk-in freezer and coolers.
- Install night curtains.

WATER HEATING AND PIPE INSULATION

- Install EPA approved WaterSource® flow restrictors and aerators.
- Install pipe insulation and a water heater blanket.
- Repair all leaks.
- Remove scale.

OPERATIONS

- Support your Green Team.
- Use 'Green' cleaners and insecticides.
- Install timers on your copy machine and vending machines.

LIGHTING

Figure 3. Pigtail CFLs are not for every application. Globe-shaped CFLs are available for specialty lamps and designer fixtures like this one. Photo by author. All rights reserved.

Start with replacing just five barely burning incandescent lamps with CFLs. Immediately replace the five incandescent light bulbs that burn out most often in your store with CFLs. There are CFLs (compact fluorescent lamps) for nearly any application. The CFLs last at least ten times longer which significantly reduces your labor installation costs and generates a nearly instant return. Next, use CFLs to replace other lamps as they fail. Special low-temperature CFL lamps are especially long-lived in freezers and coolers and can save you up to $50 per lamp each year. Replacing six 75-watt incandescent lamps in your checkstands with 23 watt CFLs will save up to $350 per year. The higher cost of the lamps is easily offset by the longer life and the labor saved by not continually replacing them. Tip: Don't buy the cheap CFLs. They don't last. Energy Star® rated lamps are definitely worth the extra money. They will live up to your long life expectations. The downside of CFL lamps is the tiny amount of mercury inside. Since mercury is now classified as a hazardous material, the disposal is more difficult. Most people feel that the CFL's negatives are far outweighed by the low operating cost, long life, dimmability and efficacy (brightness, measured in lumens per watt). Note: The CFL pictured above is the wrong application. The correct CFL for this type of decorative fixture has a globe exterior, not a pigtail.

Clean light fixtures and lamps. Your store team probably already keeps the lamps and reflectors on your cold cases and freezer doors clean and polished. Next time you have your ceiling lamps changed out, make sure the contractor also properly cleans the reflectors. Just having clean reflectors or light fixtures can brighten your store by 10 to 20%.

Install exterior timers. If you don't have a properly programmed EMS lighting control system, replace the old, worn or malfunctioning pin-timers for your parking lot and other exterior lighting. This will save wasting electricity during the day and creating light pollution at night. Note: If you are plagued with occasional power outages, invest in a solid-state timer backed up by a rechargeable battery so you don't have to reset it after every electrical incident.

Replace mercury vapor lights. Mercury vapor lights are such notorious energy hogs that the federal government has outlawed their manufacture. There are two good replacement options. 1) High Pressure Sodium Vapor (HPSV) lamps for outside with a rated life of over 24,000 hours. 2) In applications that don't require good color definition use Pulse Start Metal Halide lamps with a rated life of 30,000 hours.

Install occupancy sensors in all closed rooms. Timers on interior rooms work well for most applications, but occupancy sensors work better. They can be adjusted to go dark as soon as motion stops or a number of minutes later.

Occupancy sensors are most effective in offices, closets, supply rooms, machine rooms, rest rooms, walk-in boxes and freezers. A combination motion/infrared sensor works well for rest rooms since they react to both movement and to heat. Installing low temperature sensors in your walk-in coolers and freezers can save you about $450.00 each with a less than one year payback. Your savings will be even greater if you also install LED lamps. See the chart below for other potential savings.

ENERGY- SAVING POTENTIAL WITH OCCUPANCY SENSORS

APPLICATION	ENERGY SAVINGS
PRIVATE OFFICES	13 TO 50%
OPEN SPACE OFFICES	20 TO 25%
REST ROOMS	30 TO 90%
HALLWAYS/CORRIDORS	30 TO 80%
STORAGE AREAS	45 TO 80%
MEETING ROOMS	22 TO 65%
CONFERENCE ROOMS	45 TO 65%
WAREHOUSES	50 TO 75%

Note: These figures represent maximum savings under optimum saving conditions.

Replace neon and accent lighting with LED (Light Emitting Diode) lamps. Old exterior signage is typically illuminated by neon. Replacing the illumination elements with the new generation LED lights reduces your electrical usage by up to 80%. Inside the store, LED lights work well as track light accents or to inexpensively light up over-the-door emergency exit signs.

Install 'second generation' T-8 lamps. Suppose you were wise enough to have already replaced your T-12 lamps with T-8's a few years ago and you are now due for a lamp change-out. Make sure that the new lamps being installed are 'second generation' T-8 lamps. Lamp technology is evolving so fast that the new ones will save you about 20% more than the ones you are using now. If you still have T-12 lamps, replacing them with the newer T-8's and electronic ballast combination will multiply your savings.

Replace yellow or hazy lenses, diffusers and globes. Your image with both your customers and employees is the best reason for having clean, clear lenses, diffusers and light globes. Saving money is the second reason. Retrofitting can save you money if the new (or clean) fixtures allow you to install a lower wattage lamp while maintaining the same light output.

Buy only Energy Star® rated lamps. Energy Star® lamps are meticulously tested by third party agencies for quality and to verify advertised service life. Note: The advertised rated lamp service life (typically just called lamp life) is the amount of time it takes for 50% of a large test sample to burn out under standard conditions.

HVAC

Install timers to shut down non-essential systems during off hours. Install timers or setback programmable thermostats to shut down unneeded A/C systems during non-business hours or holidays. (Typical night setting temperatures are: cool to 90° F and heat to 55° F.) In most stores, you can adjust the A/C schedule to activate itself an hour before opening or shut down an hour before closing. For an even better alternative to timers, see "Programmable Thermostats" on page fifty.

Set economizers properly. An efficient economizer requires reliable sensors, actuators and damper mechanisms. Economizers are one of the most energy-saving parts of your air conditioning system. They are also the part that is most often disabled or compromised. A recent survey showed that only 10% of the test sample economizers were working properly eighteen months after installation. Make sure that your HVAC service includes inspection, lubrication and repair of the A/C economizers to maximize the benefit of "free cooling." When your outside air temperature and humidity are lower than the inside air (i.e. at night) your A/C unit shuts down and the economizer takes over. Since it is only a fan unit and doesn't actually cool the air, it lowers your A/C bill by about 30%.

Create and carefully follow a preventative maintenance schedule. Have all your filters changed every three months. Belts and bearings should be inspected and serviced as needed at the same time. Pay particular attention to cleaning your condenser coils and fan blades and calibrating your humidity sensors. Your contractor should also check refrigerant levels, verify current drawn (amps.), check for duct leaks and make sure that all the dampers are operating as designed. See Appendix E for a more comprehensive sample vendor PM (Preventative Maintenance) checklist.

Pretreat cooling tower water. Pretreating the water that feeds your cooling tower eliminates most of the scaling on your transpiration fins and noticeably increases the life and efficiency of your A/C unit. If you already have a water pretreating system, make sure a qualified contractor is properly maintaining it on a set schedule and that it is not wasting water.

Remove scale from heat exchange units. If and when scaling does appear, make sure removing it is an important part of your preventative maintenance scope of work.

Replace worn or cracked weather stripping and seal up all holes. Cracked or broken weather stripping is an ongoing conditioned air leak in your store. Like from a window that never closes, either your cool air or your high cost heat is escaping to the outside. If your windows or doors rattle, your weather stripping is probably deteriorating. Besides the leaks to the outside, any conditioned air being blown into an unconditioned space is costing you money, too. Search out and seal any drywall holes into your back room or machine room. (Tip: Foam board and spray foam work for most repair applications.) Your acoustic ceiling is a temperature barrier between your air conditioned store and the sun-baked roof deck. Replacing a few missing or damaged ceiling tiles is more than an aesthetic issue, it saves you money.

Install reflective tint on windows. There are dozens of different varieties of reflective window tinting that can help you lower your A/C cost by redirecting the sun's heat away from your building. At the same time, in winter, it bounces the heat back inside. Some manufacturers claim that 100 square feet of the correct tinting can replace one ton of air conditioning. Tip: Check with your property manager and local authorities to make sure there are no restrictions or ordinances.

Use portable space heaters or fans in enclosed rooms. In closed rooms, especially offices, it is far more economical to use a space heater or fan to help condition the air rather than adjusting the building A/C unit. Comfort is a function of temperature, humidity and air movement but "comfortable" is an ambiguous perception that is defined differently and debated by everyone. Simple fans can negate a temperature increase of 5°. Remember that a 1° change in temperature can lower your A/C cost by up to 2%. Also note that in a typical food store nearly 30% of your total annual electric bill is directly related to your A/C.

Seal and insulate A/C ducts in unconditioned areas. One of the biggest causes of run-away A/C costs are damaged air conditioning ducts leaking expensive conditioned air into intentionally unconditioned areas of your store. This is especially true in older facilities where the ducts are hidden above the ceiling. However, most damage is found in backroom or mezzanine areas where miscellaneous equipment and old fixtures are stacked against the air ducts. Tip: Look for a dust build-up as an indication of an air leak.

Install ceiling fans in receiving. Many older stores with high bay back room storage have non-functional ceiling fans up tight against the exposed roof deck. These are designed to drive any heat collecting at the ceiling back down to the floor. They are particularly effective when situated over a walk-in freezer or cooler door.

Install door sweeps on exterior doors. The health department already typically requires door sweeps on your exterior doors. Saving energy dollars is just another good reason to comply.

REFRIGERATION

Adjust defrost controls. Depending on your store type, nearly 50% of your total energy bill can be for refrigeration. The power consumed by overworked compressors contributes a large part of this expense. Based on the recommendations of your refrigeration contractor, have your defrost cycles reset to a minimum and scheduled to avoid demand charges. (Myth: Frost on product indicates that another defrost cycle should be added. Truth: Frost usually indicates that the defrost is running too long, clogged drains, air leaks or other issues. Adding another defrost will simply increase the problem and your energy consumption.)

Carefully follow your Refrigeration System Preventative Maintenance schedule. With your refrigeration contractor's help, create a PM (preventative maintenance) schedule that covers all your refrigeration equipment. Include coils and lubrication. Make sure that your maintenance contractor actually does the work. Quality time spent with him as he explains exactly what he did during each visit pays off immediately. Verify that your refrigeration is charged properly. Either undercharged or overcharged compromises your refrigeration efficiency by 5 to 20%. See Appendix E for a sample PM checklist.

Figure 4. The dollar bill test on a properly gasketed frozen food doorframe. Photo by author. All rights reserved.

Perform a dollar bill test on all freezer and cooler doors. (It shouldn't slip out!) If a dollar bill slips easily between your door seals, you need to replace them. Some municipalities and/or utilities will rebate a portion of this cost. Check for cracked, smashed or bent door gaskets around each freezer and cooler door. Typically, the seals at the bottom of the door wear out first because of your crew standing on them as they stock product. Also pay attention to accumulating frost on the doors, which is a sign that your seals are bad or that you might need a new door heater.

Service walk-in boxes annually. Walk-in boxes are less prone to breakdown than sales-floor refrigerated cases and are often ignored. Be sure to have the coils cleaned and serviced as part of your regular PM protocol, especially the medium temp coolers. Also check for leaks around the doors caused by cracked or missing door gaskets and misaligned doorframes. Most cooler and freezer box damage is the result of poorly driven pallet jacks, so check the caulked seams and joints at the floor-line, too.

Install anti-sweat heater controls on frozen food doors. The anti-sweat function that keeps the glass on your frozen doors clear doesn't need to be operational 24 hours a day. Adjust the system controls to take that circuit off-line when the store is closed.

Install insulation on bare refrigeration lines. Refrigeration line insulation wears, weathers and rots with age. At a minimum, have your refrigeration contractor replace worn and/or saturated insulation on all suction lines within six feet of the compressor rack. There are rebates available in many areas to help defray some of this cost.

Install swinging doors to cooling areas. Every barrier that you can maintain to keep your cold air from escaping from your chilled prep areas to your sales floor or back room is money in the bank. Keep the swinging doors to your prep areas in good repair with the seals intact.

Replace T-12 case lighting with T-8 lamps or LED lighting. Many energy-conscious managers replaced all their T-12 ceiling lights with more efficient T-8 or T-5 lamps but forget the long row of lights (sometimes double row) on their open front cold cases. Replacing them with LED lights is an even better choice.

Install automatic door closers on walk-in freezers and coolers. An automatic door closer is a simple mechanism that attaches to the top of your cooler or freezer doorframe. It activates to pull the door shut when the door swings within one inch of closing.

Install night curtains. Night curtains are like a cold-impervious shade that you pull down at night on all of your open-front cases to contain the refrigerated air. In only six hours per night, they can reduce your cold case power consumption by 12.5% and repay their installation cost in as little as six months. Also, studies have shown that closing the night curtains on your produce wet racks extends your produce shelf life.

Figure 5. Night curtains. One of the fastest ROI upgrades available for your store. Photograph courtesy of SUPERVALU INC. © 2009. All rights reserved. Reprinted with permission.

WATER HEATING AND PIPE INSULATION

Install EPA approved WaterSource® flow restrictors and aerators. Besides the obvious cost of just purchasing your water, there are two hidden charges. 1) The cost to heat it. 2) The cost to dump it into your sewer. Don't waste water! EPA approved WaterSource® aerators and flow retarders are quick, inexpensive, easy to install and can reduce your water consumption by up to 30%.

Install pipe insulation and a water heater blanket. Most heat loss from your water heater occurs within the first three to six feet of the "out" pipe. Insulate as much as possible, but definitely the first six feet. Wrapping your water heater with a heat blanket is a good idea both at your store and at home. Water heater blankets are easy to install and are available at your local hardware store.

Repair all leaks. Compared to electricity, your water cost seems so miniscule that's it's hardly worth bothering about, but leaking or dripping faucets can waste hundreds of gallons of water every day. Throwing away cold water is bad enough but a fast flowing hot water leak will quickly cost you more than a visit from your plumber.

Remove scale. If your store is cursed with high mineral-content water, make sure that the accompanying scale is removed as a regular part of your preventative maintenance protocol. There are a number of eco-safe commercial cleaners available that will safely dissolve the buildup.

See **awarenessideas.com** for more examples to help your sustainability program.

2.25 x 4.25 red and green light switch cover

3" diameter dark blue equipment sticker

6" diameter sticker dark blue on white

12" x 18" poster two tone blue

OPERATIONS

Support your Green Team. A good "Green Team" can save you thousands of dollars each year. Support your team's efforts and enthusiasm by creating a signage package that effectively spreads their environment-saving message. This is easier than it sounds. Long before the environment became front-page news, awarenessideas.com (800 875 – 1725) created a number of energy-related programs for Fortune 500 companies. Based on those successes, they built a collection of thousands of energy related posters, signs, decals and other clever ways to keep your money-saving message moving forward. Check out their web site. You will be amazed at how many different and unique ways they can inexpensively support your Green Team while contributing to your bottom line. Above are just a few of the huge selection of signs, posters, decals and other items that they have available.

Use 'Green' cleaners and insecticides. The EPA Environmentally Preferable Product Information list is your most up-to-date source of information about government approved cleaners and insecticides. Both your ecology-minded customers and employees will appreciate knowing that you are using cleaners and insecticides that are environmentally safe and listed among the EPA's Environmentally Preferred Products. The payback is more in public relations than in dollars, but well worth the trouble.

Install timers on your copy machine and vending machines. A timer to shut off your copy machine overnight will only save you a little money, the real energy hogs are your soda vending machines. The big outdoor type work hard all night to refrigerate a lot of interior space just to keep a few sodas cold that no one will likely buy until morning. Soda vendors are working to get their machines retrofitted with both sensors and timers. Approach them first to see if there are machines available. If not, get a timer, then go after a possible rebate.

CHAPTER THREE

Investing In Your Green Store

It's time to get serious about saving money and energy. Depending on your store location, many of the upgrades listed below have ROIs of between six months and three years. Sustainability isn't an all or nothing proposition. It is simply a slow-growing philosophy that is the right thing to do both globally and for your bottom line. Even when the technology and the return on investment are well tested and proven, there is no reason to commit huge amounts of capital to a big remodel. Start with three or four fast payback projects that your customers and store team will instantly notice and appreciate. Then slip in a couple high ROI projects that are completely invisible like new ECM fan motors or HVAC motor upgrades.

Don't forget the EPA estimate that $1 dollar in energy saving is equivalent to increasing your sales by $59. Many grocers have found that reducing costs by reducing their energy consumption gives them a competitive edge. They don't have to work nearly as hard for sales when their store saves them a bag full of cash every day.

As you can see on the following chart, the highest energy expense categories (in descending order by cost) are refrigeration, lighting and A/C. Lighting is the most obvious, so start there, but don't skip refrigeration, that's where a small spend can have the most profitable impact.

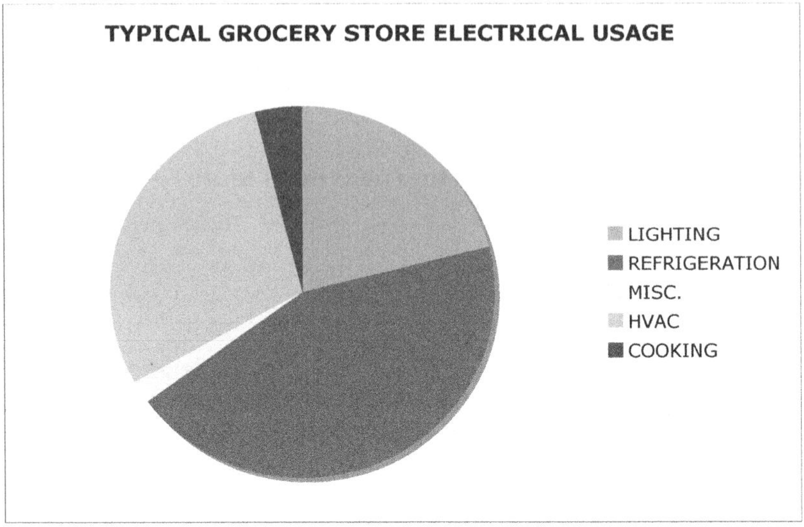

COMMISSIONING AND RETROCOMMISSIONING

You can't fix what you don't know is broken! Or, more appropriately, you can't manage what you don't measure. Too many marginally profitable stores limp along burdened by huge monthly energy bills and don't even have an inkling that anything is wrong. More importantly, they don't see how easily their profitability can be dramatically improved. Depending on your store, its age and how poorly your equipment works together, commissioning can net you an instant 10 to 20% reduction on your energy bill. It could change a seldom-profitable store into a consistent winner.

Commissioning is a very methodical process that verifies that all the store's equipment, especially in interdependent systems, is operating together as designed. This review should include rooftop A/C units, lighting, alarms, fans, hoods and your energy management system.

Retrocommissioning is simply the process of commissioning an existing building. It's a documented process by an experienced contractor focused on balancing mechanical equipment, lighting and the related controls. The results can include improved indoor air quality and lighting, comfort, energy management controls and resource efficiency. Most importantly, retrocommissioning exposes operational and maintenance improvements that can be inexpensive to install and often have a payback less than two years.

The most common simple-to-fix problems uncovered during the retrocommissioning process include: miscalibrated or improper refrigeration set points, nonfunctional humidity sensors, poorly timed lighting, bypassed refrigeration controls that ignore energy saving potential, inoperative fan motors and broken belts.

Retrocommissioning should be among your top ten energy-saving upgrades and definitely part of every remodel. The paybacks are too significant to pass up. Go to www.aztec-energy.com for advise on all your commissioning and recommissioning questions.

Easy Savings Checklist

LIGHTING

- Replace all T-12 fluorescent lamps with T-8 or T-5 lamps.
- Replace all magnetic ballasts with electronic ballasts.
- Install dimmable ballasts.
- Install bi-level switching on sales floor.
- Install energy-efficient lighting in frozen food cases.
- Install skylights with photo-sensors.
- Install HID (High Intensity Discharge) lamps or high bay fluorescent lamps in warehouse.

- Control daylighting and optimize daylight harvesting.
- Install LED case lighting and accent lighting.
- Replace parking lot lighting with LED lamps.
- Install LED (Light Emitting Diode) lights in EXIT signs.
- Paint walls a light color.
- Install motion detectors on exterior wall pack fixtures for when your store is closed.
- Change out lighting in groups.

HVAC

- Install economizers.
- Install automatic shut-off devices.
- Install Carbon Dioxide sensors.
- Install adjustable speed drives on HVAC equipment.
- Balance air handler.
- Install an EMS system capable of separately controlling lighting, HVAC and refrigeration.
- Install programmable thermostats.
- Install power factor increasing devices.
- Install variable air volume system.
- Ventilate internal heat sources to the outside.
- Install multi-pane windows.
- Install special window coverings and/or awnings.
- Install low-emissivity windows.
- Install attic fans.

- Install a light colored, preferably snow white, roof membrane.
- Research landscaping options.
- Purchase Energy Star® rated equipment.

REFRIGERATION

- Install ECM (Electronically Commutated Motors) motors.
- Install strip curtains.
- Install glass doors on refrigerated cases.
- Install anti-sweat controls.
- Add floating head pressure and suction pressure controls to refrigerated units.
- Install reach-in freezer cases with no-heat doors.

WATER AND WATER HEATING

- Preheat hot water with a heat recovery system.
- Install water-efficient faucets and toilets.
- Install instant-hot water heaters.
- Install Energy Star® rated water heater.

OUTSIDE

- Change to a drip irrigation system.
- Plant greenscaping, xeriscaping.
- Utilize renewable energy sources.

OPERATIONS

- Don't forget your Green Team.
- Buy only Energy Star® rated office equipment.

Checklist Suggestions and Tips

LIGHTING

Replace all T-12 fluorescent lamps with T-8 or T-5 lamps. Replacing all of your old fashioned fat T-12 lamps can be pricey but instantly worthwhile. T-8's and T-5's are thinner in diameter, more efficient, have a higher efficacy (brightness, measured in lumens per watt) and render truer color than T-12 lamps. Tip: Ask for "second generation" T-8 lamps because they use 20% less electricity than the original T-8s. Depending on the ballasts, they burn 20% to 40% fewer watts and last longer. Since the smaller diameter lamps are also brighter, you can use fewer lamps to get the same light saturation. You gain further, but harder to document, savings because the T-8's and T-5's generate less heat and therefore reduce your A/C costs.

Replace all magnetic ballasts with electronic ballasts. Changing to T8's necessitates replacing the old (first used in 1939) magnetic ballasts with new electronic ballasts as part of a system. The combination of new lamps and complementing ballasts almost doubles your savings. Even though your existing ballasts may have a number of remaining service years, it will pay to replace them. The newest generation ballasts are virtually flicker-free and burn up to 30% less energy. Tip: Make sure that your old ballasts are disposed of properly. If they contain PCBs, Polychlorinated Biphenyls, a government banned hazardous material, it should be noted on the label.

Install dimmable ballasts. If you have (or are going to install) skylights, then dimmable ballasts are a must. The light brightness (efficacy) is controlled by light sensors mounted in the skylights. Better dimmable ballasts can lower light levels using such minute incremental changes that your customers will never notice. Note: Fluorescent lamps usually die from cathode failure caused by turning them on and off. Since the electrical usage is so minimal, it pays you to dim the lamps to about 10% but never to turn them off.

Install bi-level light switching on sales floor. In some skylight-enhanced lighting situations, the quantity of dimmable ballasts that are needed is cost prohibitive. It may be more prudent to rewire a long line of T-8 ceiling lights to an A/B configuration. Simply stated, a row of lights can be either on or off (A or B) but not dimmed. Since each row is controlled separately with different activation/deactivation points, they can be turned off without as much impact on your customers. The downside of a photometer activated A/B configuration is that fluorescent lamps typically die as a result of cathode failure due to being turned off and on too many times. Look into the long-term cost of each alternative before committing to the work.

Figure 6. Photo by Hussmann Refrigeration. Reprinted with permission. All rights reserved

Install energy-efficient lighting in frozen food cases. Because of the quickly evolving technology, there are a number of LED lighting alternatives that have recently come to market. In test stores where they were installed in frozen cases, certain packaging colors in the blue and purple areas of the color spectrum appear much more vibrant. An added plus is that LED lights generate far less heat than the old style fluorescent lamps so the freezer temperature setting could be raised several degrees while still maintaining the same product temperatures.

Install skylights with photo-sensors. Unlike the original clear-domed versions, the latest generation of skylights diffuses light over a wide area necessitating fewer skylights to create the same effective light density. Both products and people look better under natural light plus there is mounting evidence that sales increase and employee turnover decreases in day-lit stores. Depending on the season, when skylights are used in conjunction with a properly controlled lighting system, daylighting can reduce your daily sales floor lighting cost by up to 50%.

Figure 7. Skylight Retrofit. Photograph courtesy of SUPERVALU INC. © 2009. All rights reserved. Reprinted with permission.

Install HID (High Intensity Discharge) lamps or high bay fluorescent lamps in warehouse. Because these lamps can be so bright, they are best used for lighting large areas from high ceilings. Since the new generation ceramic halide lamps are far more color accurate, they are occasionally used as accent lighting in large retail stores. Their typical usage is in garages, warehouses, stockrooms, and for exterior safety and security lighting.

Control daylighting and optimize daylight harvesting. Even in stores without skylights, proper lighting controls can significantly lower your electrical usage. Depending on the direction that your store faces and the amount of glass on your store-front, you can turn off or dim as much as a third of your ceiling lights during part of the day. Obviously, you should dim your sales floor lighting to 50% or less for night stocking after the store closes.

Install LED case lighting and accent lighting. New potential applications for LED lighting are evolving every day. LED lamps burn cooler, and look brighter using up to 65% less power and last over ten times longer than incandescent lamps. Their estimated useful life is unaffected by lower temperatures so they are well suited for use in both walk-in and sales floor freezer lighting. Their directional versatility and low-cost light intensity make them an obvious choice for any cold case presentation, including meat and produce. There are hundreds of stores across the country that have now successfully and profitably switched to 100% LED lighting. An added bonus is that, unlike CFLs, they don't use mercury with its hazardous materials issues.

Replace parking lot lighting with LED lamps. LED lights are also great for parking lots because of their accurately defined angle of illumination. They are the perfect answer for situations that are particularly sensitive to light pollution like a discontented neighbor's back yard or bedroom window.

Install LED (Light Emitting Diode) lights in EXIT signs. Typical incandescent EXIT sign lamps consume 20 to 50 watts with an anticipated life of only 2000 to 5000 hours. A single sign could cost as much as $60/year. An LED lamp burns only 1.5 to 2.0 watts with an up to 40-year estimated useful life. Most people generally ignore emergency exit signs except for that once-in-a-lifetime situation when we need them the most or during a fire inspection. It's cheap insurance to install new LED lamps once and know that they will most likely remain operative for the rest of your career. Tip: Many utilities are offering significant rebates on LED exit lights. Even without a rebate the payback is less than one year.

Figure 8. LED illuminated EXIT sign. Photo by author. All rights reserved.

Paint walls a light color. Dark colors suck up light. The lighter the color that your wall, ceiling and floors are, the less light you need. High reflectivity guarantees a lower lighting cost, so don't use a matte (flat) finish paint.

Install motion detectors on exterior wall pack fixtures for when your store is closed. A generation ago, exterior wall pack lighting was installed for aesthetic reasons. Depending on safety and security issues in your neighborhood, it might be worthwhile to install sensors on each fixture allowing them to be off each night only when no one is near.

Change out lighting in groups. Both incandescent and fluorescent lamps typically lose 20 to 30% of their brightness over their service life. Compared to the labor to install them, lamps are very inexpensive. Replacing all the lamps in an entire lighting system (i.e. all the case lamps or all the ceiling lamps) saves labor, maintains the design lighting standard and doesn't over-stress any ballasts with dying lamps. When changing out lamps, consider the following: initial lamp cost, anticipated useful life, energy consumption per lamp and maintenance cost. Note: Make sure that your old lamps are disposed of properly.

HVAC

Install economizers. An economizer is an add-on to typical package-unit A/C systems that saves money by providing free cooling. Through the use of dampers and automatic temperature-activated and humidity-dewpoint activated controls, the quantity of fresh air entering the space can be adjusted. In locations where the outside temperatures and humidity are nearly equal, this saves the cost of conditioning the air by not passing it through the A/C unit but instead simply pumping fresh air into the space.

Install automatic shut-off devices. Some elements of your EMS controlled A/C system are better handled by simple automatic shut-offs. (Bathroom fans are a prime example.) It is far less expensive to tie your bathroom fans to a motion-activated light switch than to try to manage them through your EMS system.

Install Carbon Dioxide sensors. Traditional HVAC systems import fresh air based on an assumed occupancy. Newer technology allows your A/C unit to react efficiently to the Carbon Dioxide concentration in your space. This type of sensor is particularly effective in seldom-used meeting rooms. The net result is both a more energy-efficient operation and better air quality.

Install adjustable speed drives on HVAC equipment. Adjustable Speed Drives, ASDs, (also known as Adjustable Frequency Drives, AFDs, and Variable Speed Drives, VSDs or Flow Modulators) are used to adjust the speed on your HVAC unit's fan, blower, compressor and pump motors to reduce your electrical usage by matching the fluctuating loads. Since most HVAC units are oversized, running them at a reduced load extends the life of the motors and all the driven equipment. ASDs can reduce A/C electrical usage by up to 30%.

Balance air handler. Have your qualified contractor balance all aspects of your air handling system including office, service departments, storage areas, hoods and restrooms. This should be done as part of your retrocommissioning process. Properly adjusting your building envelope pressurization to keep high humidity air outside helps lower both your refrigeration and HVAC energy costs.

Install an EMS system capable of separately controlling lighting, HVAC, and refrigeration. If you don't already have an EMS system capable of controlling all aspects of your energy savings, look into installing one as soon as possible. EMS benefits include: reduced energy costs, improved facility management, reduced manpower requirements and faster and better response to emergency and trouble situations. A properly tuned and implemented EMS system typically reduces your electrical costs by 10 to 20%.

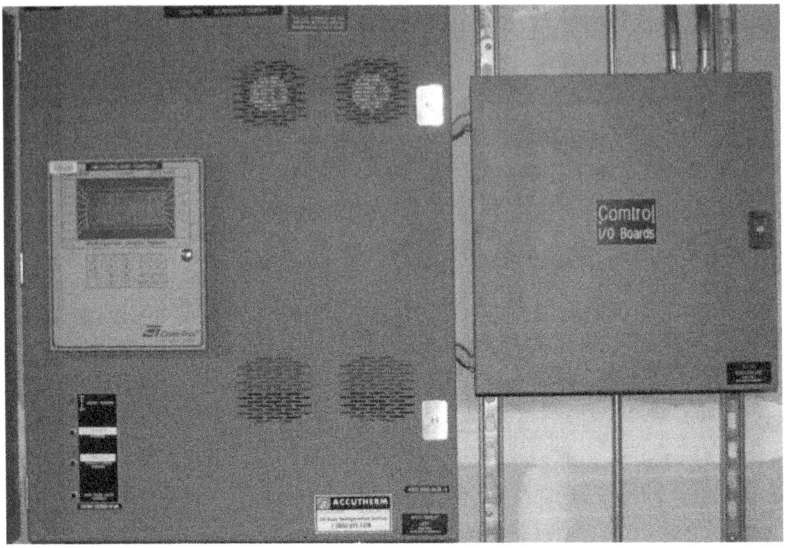

Figure 9. Comtrol EMS system. Photo by author. Printed with permission. All rights reserved.

Install programmable thermostats. One of the easiest and most effective upgrades, if you can't afford a complete EMS system, is to install programmable thermostats. Your store temperature needs to be both customer friendly and energy-conservative. Make sure that your new thermostats are not installed near a heat or cold source or in direct sunlight and that they are properly calibrated as you install them. Note: Raising your thermostat setting a single degree can save you 2% of your A/C cost per year. Lowering the heat setting 1° can save 3% of your heating cost.

Install power factor increasing devices. In an electric power system, a load with a low power factor draws more current than a load with a high power factor for the same amount of useful power transferred. This is only important in areas where the utility company charges a penalty to stores with a low power factor. A high Power Factor is worth considering in some lighting situations but really pays for itself when replacing motors or when it is a major element on your energy bill.

Install variable air volume system. A Variable Air Volume System (VAV unit) distributes a variable volume of conditioned air from an air-handling unit. It is controlled by individual thermostats to provide fresh air to specific zones. The zones are self-adapting and defined by the occupancy levels (as measured by the Carbon Dioxide concentrations) or simply controlled by occupancy sensors.

Ventilate internal heat sources to the outside. Your deli and other kitchen areas generate too much heat to try and overcome by pumping in extra conditioned air. This heat is nearly impossible to reuse and not worth the expense. A simple exhaust fan on the roof will dissipate the heat at a much lower cost.

Install multi-pane windows. Double or triple-paned windows have the highest payback only in the most intemperate areas. They make the most sense when installed as part of the original building. Except in the harshest environments, cost wise, they are hard to justify as a retrofit energy-saver. The payback is simply too long.

Install special window coverings and/or awnings. Often a cheaper and more versatile alternative to multi-pane windows is to cover or somehow shade your existing windows. Horizontal or vertical blinds or window graphics are good energy compromises. Awnings create predictable shade to save energy, but don't skimp on the up-front cost with cheap canvas or plastic and don't forget to factor in the cost of periodically cleaning them. Window tinting is an even cheaper option. These films dramatically reduce building heat gain in the summer time and "bounce" the heat back into your store in the winter. Check with your property manager and local authorities to see if there are any restrictions.

Install low-emissivity windows. High performance, gas filled, double-paned "low emissivity" (Low-E) windows are quickly becoming a standard in the industry. They insulate as well as triple-paned glass but cost less. These windows are an excellent choice as new equipment, but not as a quick ROI retrofit.

Install attic fans. Since a store's warm air rises to an already sun-baked attic, add attic fans to remove the heated air. Because of the potential long payback, this is a poor choice unless you are replacing the roof at the same time.

Install a light-colored, preferably snow-white, roof membrane. A new roof is a huge capital expense; so when the time comes for a replacement, look into a TPO roof. They are bright white and reflect sunlight more efficiently than any other type of roof. In many areas, they are also cheaper than any other roof type. Depending on your location, a white roof can reduce your cooling energy cost by 15 to 20%. Tip: Make sure you hire an experienced, competent, financially stable installer to support the TPO's long warranty.

Research landscape options. Depending on your common area maintenance restrictions, you may be able to plant trees or other foliage to strategically shade your building and minimize solar gain. Shading the south facing wall will have the largest effect on the temperature of your building.

Purchase Energy Star® rated equipment. Equipment manufacturers jump through a lot of hoops to gain an Energy Star® rating for their products. Only the best make it. When you consider the overall life-cycle cost and the number of years you will enjoy lower utility bills, it is worth any extra up front cost. With Energy Star® rated equipment, you get more work for the same amount of energy, less required run time, less down time, less maintenance and less heat generation. There are free savings calculators available on the Energy Star® website to compute your potential savings.

REFRIGERATION

Install ECM (Electronically Commutated Motors) motors. Electronically commutated motors (also known as DC brushless motors or AC induction motors) are the highest performing and efficient motors available for use as fan motors. Replacing the fan motors in all your cold cases and the coils in your walk-in boxes can reduce your fan motor electrical usage by nearly 80%. In one test store, the net savings were close to $40,000 with a ROI of less than one year. The following chart summarizes the resulting savings from the installation of 348 ECM motors in a 40,000 square foot grocery store. Replacing existing fan motors with ECM motors is one of the most energy-efficient upgrades you can make to your refrigeration system. The payback here was less than one year.

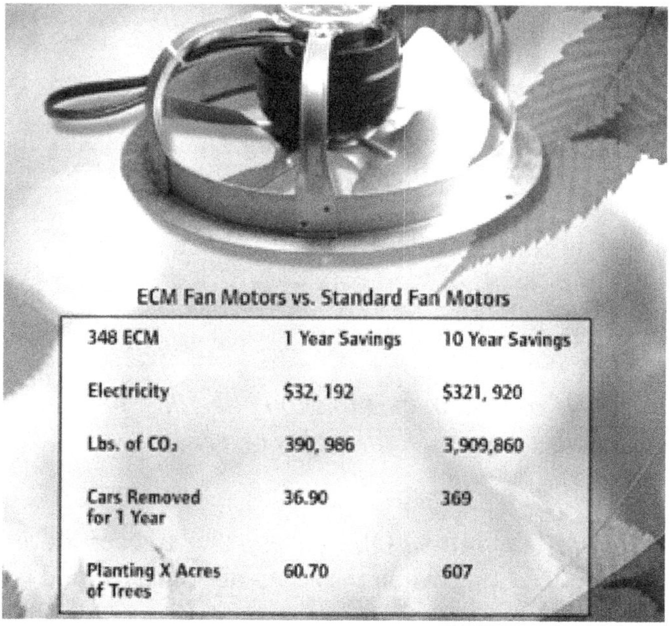

ECM Fan Motors vs. Standard Fan Motors

348 ECM	1 Year Savings	10 Year Savings
Electricity	$32, 192	$321, 920
Lbs. of CO_2	390, 986	3,909,860
Cars Removed for 1 Year	36.90	369
Planting X Acres of Trees	60.70	607

Figure 10. ECM fan motor comparison. Graphic by Hussmann Refrigeration. Reprinted with permission.

Figure 11. If your strip curtains look like this, please replace them.. Photo by author.

Install strip curtains. Of course, the freezer door strip curtains are irritating when they slap at your face and back as you walk through, but they can save you a couple thousand dollars a year by reducing ambient air infiltration into your freezer by up to 75%. Besides the freezer, they should be installed on all your walk-in boxes. Strip curtains have one of the fastest paybacks of any energy-saving equipment that you can install. The strip curtains shown here were disabled by a disgruntled night stocker.

Install glass doors on refrigerated cases. Tests recently performed by SCE (Southern California Edison) showed an over 50% reduction in refrigeration cost after glass doors were retrofitted on open front cold cases. Until glass doors are federally mandated, there will always be a debate over whether the doors restrict sales or slow down stocking. Other data shows that any potential loss in sales is more than compensated by the reduced energy usage.

Figure 12. New energy-saving retrofit glass doors on formerly open-front egg case. Photo by author. Printed with permission. All rights reserved.

Install anti-sweat controls. Many anti-sweat door heaters run 24 hours per day with no controls which waste energy in two ways. First; a third of the electricity that you use to heat the doors is at night after you close. Second; your compressors, which account for 30 to 40% of your refrigeration electrical cost, have to work harder to maintain temperatures while the door heaters are on. An effective EMS system will also react to changes in humidity which may allow your door heaters to remain off during parts of the day.

Add floating head pressure and suction pressure controls to refrigerated units. Many refrigeration (compressor rack) systems are designed for worst-case scenario weather conditions with no thought to energy efficiency. Adding floating suction pressure controls and floating head suction controls can save about $20,000/year in a large format store.

Install reach-in freezer cases with no-heat doors. Cost effective no-heat doors are a recent arrival in the market place. The savings are substantial especially when installing all new cases.

WATER AND WATER HEATING

Preheat hot water with a heat recovery system. Additional energy savings can be realized if the hot gas from the refrigeration compressors is used to preheat the water going to the domestic water supply. This translates into a no-cost energy source and is not a difficult or expensive retrofit. Note: A 7.5 HP compressor can provide nearly 100% of the hot water needed in a medium-sized grocery store.

Install water-efficient faucets and toilets. The cost of water is only a small part of your total energy bill, but well worth careful scrutiny. Beyond the dollar figure on your utility statement, there is the hidden cost to heat it and the ignored cost of flushing it into the sewer system. Fixing the drips and leaks is the first and most obvious step. The more costly second step is to replace the faulty or marginal faucets and to install low water usage toilets. Careful attention to detail can reduce your water consumption by half.

Install instant-hot water heaters. Instant-hot water heaters are a perfect solution for sink locations that are remote from your master water heater (i.e. restrooms). There are a number of tankless models available that will help save both the cold water you throw away waiting for the hot water to travel to your sink and the electricity or gas you use to keep the water hot in a large tank. When you consider that you also waste the cost of heating all the hot water that is left in the pipe between the end-point sink and the hot water heater when you turn the hot water off, the cost of an instant-hot water heater becomes even more sensible. Note: There are rebates attached to many Energy Star® tankless water heaters.

Install Energy Star® rated water heater. Just as with their lighting specifications, Energy Star® has stringent requirements for the construction and working specifications of their industrial water heaters. Take the time to shop around before your water heater crashes to find a qualified Energy Star® model and a reputable installer.

OUTSIDE

Change to a drip irrigation system. With a drip irrigation system, you solve a number of problems, both ecologically and operationally. Since the entire water dispensing part of the system is underground, you have no more sprayed cars or broken sprinkler heads fountaining into your parking lot. Whereas a standard sprinkler type system delivers water with only about 60% efficiency, a drip irrigation system puts up to 95% of the supplied water exactly where it is needed. If you can tap into your city's non-potable water system, you will save even more.

Plant greenscaping, xeriscaping. Xeriscaping is the technical term for utilizing a dry landscape design with water conservation as its primary objective. Typically, you plant drought resistant native plants that are already acclimated to both local climate and insect predation. Greenscaping also includes the concept of planting on the south, east and west sides of building to create shade that cools your building envelope to reduce your A/C cost.

Utilize renewable energy sources. The renewable energy field is evolving exponentially. Information that is only a month old is often outdated and equipment that was manufactured only six months past is already obsolete. The most exciting new technologies applicable to grocery store operations, as of this writing, are LED lighting and Photo Voltaic Power Generation. For an overview of some of the best updated information about what is new in energy that would be best for your store, see the on-line resources listed in Appendix D.

OPERATIONS

Don't forget your Green Team. In the first two chapters we stressed the importance of your Green Team. Sustainability is too big of an issue to tackle alone. Take advantage of every resource possible to make the job easier for you and your associates. Using the expertise available at awarenessideas.com, you and your team can create dozens of high-visibility, energy-saving programs that will keep your message alive and growing. Considering the profit potential and the positive environmental impact, sustainability can easily become one of the most important money-saving programs ever started in your store.

Install only Energy Star® rated office equipment. When you look at saving money and energy through your office equipment, you only have two real choices: 1) Turn it off! 2) Buy Energy Star® rated equipment. Manufacturers all over the world are rushing to get an Energy Star® rating on the equipment they sell. Fortunately, there is nothing automatic about the approval process so spending a little extra money for better equipment quickly pays for itself in saved electricity. The DOE (Department of Energy) through their Energy Star® program maintains a growing list of the best energy efficient equipment available for your office. Many of the listed items carry rebates, so don't miss out when they are available.

SUMMARY

There is no question that the cost of energy is going to continue to increase and that the government will be more deeply involved. By using the techniques that we have outlined in this book, you can side step the attack on your bottom line and be ahead of the environmental mandates. It is nice to know you are helping to reduce your company's overall carbon footprint and doing the right thing ecologically, but the reality is that you need to make a profit. You can cut labor or expenses. Saving energy in the ways we described can do both.

If you are only going to "take away" one upgrade from all that we have discussed in this book, make it TURN IT OFF! It's a simple message that is easy to sell to your team. Start with how to stop wasting light energy. Whether you use just light switches or a sophisticated EMS system, everyone can relate to turning off a light. Air conditioning and refrigeration are harder to comprehend but, since they account for over 70% of your energy cost, once your team gets on your program, the savings are huge.

We have shown you over 101 obvious and measurable ways to save both money and energy in your grocery store. A change in environmental philosophy and buying into a few carefully chosen upgrades can reduce your energy consumption (and electric bill) by as much as 50%. Many of the upgrades we discussed have an ROI of less than two years, some as little as six months. Beyond the money, the unmeasured attributes include happier staff and customers who are aware of, and appreciate, your environmental sustainability contribution.

Based on the information in this book, in a recent Silver LEED certified remodel, we reduced a 50,000 square foot grocery store's annual energy expense by over $100,000. We cherry-picked the following ten fast-payback, high ROI upgrades to save money while earning the highest possible immediate return. The first two were the most important:

1. Tasking the "Green Team" to accomplish as many of the fifty Chapter One tasks as possible.
2. Retrocommissioning. (ROI varies with existing condition of the store.)
3. Skylights. (ROI = 2.2 years.)
4. Dimming Ballasts. (ROI = 3 years.)
5. Night curtains on all open-front cold cases in meat, produce and meat deli. (ROI = 6 – 9 months.)
6. ECM (Electronically Commutated Motor) motors for all frozen and refrigerated cases and walk-in box coils. (ROI = 2.0 years.)
7. LED lighting on all frozen and dairy doors, wall wash lighting, track lights and department accent lights. (ROI = 1.9 years.)
8. Strip Curtains in the walk-in freezer and dairy box. (ROI = 6 months.)

9. ASD (Adjustable Speed Drives) on selected HVAC motors. (ROI = 18 – 24 months.)
10. Retrofit glass doors onto all open front dairy cases. (ROI = 12 -18 months.)

ACKNOWLEDGEMENTS

The ideas and inspiration for all the money-saving upgrades we accomplished at the first Silver LEED certified remodel in California came from dozens of different sources. That input evolved into this book. I would like to thank the following people and companies for all their contributions both to the remodel and to what is written here. This book would not be possible without their help.

DURING THE REMODEL:

Jeff Recker – Accutherm Refrigeration. We would have never gained Siler LEED status without all his energy-saving suggestions and team support.

Kenny Yamamoto – Aztec Energy Partners. His management of the energy sub-contractors and attention to detail established a higher standard for the entire field team.

Palladeo Construction – The Design/Build construction company that rose to the LEED certification challenge that was far beyond their original scope of work. Santos Lacuesta, Nathalie Gonzalez, Maurice Garcia and Myron Thomas were the key players.

WITH THIS BOOK

CTAC – Southern California Edison's Consumer Technology Application Center. Offers dozens of free in-depth classes and seminars on all aspects of energy efficiency and energy management. Much of what is presented here, I learned or refined at CTAC. The staff at CTAC is extraordinarily knowledgeable and extremely helpful. Everyone in the Southern California energy industry should avail themselves of this SCE resource.

Nathan Wesselius, PE. – Clive Samuels and Associates. Reviewed everything written here for technical accuracy, made suggestions on presentation and content and helped me through the publication process.

Jeff Recker – Accutherm Refrigeration. Was instrumental in finding and helping me correct any misstatements and technical errors.

Dean Cromwell, Robert Eidson and Bruce Rolston – Aztec Energy Partners. Did the final refrigeration, HVAC and EMS technical reviews and verified that my comments and instructions are appropriate and helpful.

Anna McHargue – Is the very best grammar, spelling, word usage and punctuation editor that I know. Her corrections and suggestions were many and much appreciated.

APPENDIX A

GREEN TEAM CHECKLIST

DAILY

FRONT END/OFFICE

- o Turn off office lights when unoccupied.
- o Close front doors.
- o Turn off checkstand lights and motors when not in use.
- o Verify that all power strips are being properly utilized.
- o Verify supply of recycled paper for in store memos.
- o Turn off Bank lights. PM
- o Turn off copy machine. PM
- o Turn off computers and printers. PM
- o Turn off half of overhead lights at closing. PM

BACKROOM

- o Check all toilets for leaks.
- o Turn off loading dock lights.
- o Close all sales floor-to-backroom doors.
- o Close receiving doors.
- o Close compressor room doors.
- o Close walk-in freezer and cooler doors.
- o Verify proper fly fan operation.
- o Close roof hatch.
- o Turn off battery chargers.

- Turn off unnecessary backroom lighting.
- Turn off janitor room lighting.
- Turn off janitor room faucets.

SERVICE DEPARTMENTS

- Turn off hood when not in use.
- Turn down unused fryers.
- Turn off unneeded fryers and rotisserie.
- Shut off all walk-in box lights when not needed.
- Turn off unneeded proofer.
- Check for case leaks while sweeping.
- Verify that strip curtains are not propped open.
- Check all faucets and sinks for leaks.
- Check all case temperatures on a regular, defined schedule.
- Check load limits on all cold cases and freezers.
- Replace easily accessible burned out lamps.
- Verify that the proper cleaning supplies are readily available.

SERVICE DEPARTMENTS (AT CLOSING)

- Close night curtains. PM
- Turn off track and accent lights. PM
- Turn off all department lights. PM
- Turn off hot case and remote islands. PM
- Turn off donut case lighting. PM
- Turn off heat wrap station. PM
- Turn off oven. PM
- Turn off all case lights. PM
- Turn off bread slicer & photo cake machine. PM

MONTHLY

- Verify that the parking lot and exterior lighting on/off schedules match the season.
- Verify that all interior and exterior motion sensors are working properly.
- Calibrate all thermostats and set to proper temperatures.
- Vacuum all freestanding and self-contained freezer and refrigeration coils including break room and floral.
- Flush and clean ice freezer.
- Check for damage to doors, panel connections and seals on all walk-in cooler and freezer boxes.
- Clean and unblock all registers and grills.
- Clean grease filters.
- Clean stove burners.
- Inspect door sweeps on exterior doors.
- From inside, look for light leaking into your walk-in boxes through broken or cracked door gaskets.

ANNUALLY

- Clean honeycombs, drains and drain pans.
- Clean all case light reflectors.
- Inspect A/C duct for leaks especially on the mezzanine.
- Install fresh batteries in all battery-operated thermostats.
- Check all doors and windows for air leaks and damaged weather stripping.
- Remove all leaves and debris from around roof drains and gutters.
- Review your local utility and state rebate programs.
- Turn off heater pilot lights and timers in summer.

- Recalibrate broilers and ovens.
- Replace yellow or hazy lenses, diffusers and globes.
- Perform "dollar bill" test on all frozen food doors.

APPENDIX B

TERMS

- **Accent lighting** – draws attention to special features or enhances the aesthetics of both indoor and outdoor environments.
- **Adjustable Speed Drives (ASD)** - are also called variable frequency drives or variable speed drives. Their primary function is to match the motor's speed to fluctuating loads.
- **Air Conditioning** – describes the creation of both cool and warm air, not just cooled air.
- **Air Mixing Plenum** – One of the key components of your HVAC unit where the return air and the outside air intake are mixed.
- **Ambient lighting** – the general illumination in an area, both indoors and outdoors, excluding task and accent lighting.
- **Amperes (Amps)** – a measure of electrical current. An increase of either amps or volts increases wattage as follows: Watts = Volts x Amps.
- **Ballast** – a piece of electrical equipment that properly controls the current flow to both fluorescent and HID lamps.
- **Ballast Efficacy Factor (BEF)** - is used to compare lighting effectiveness between systems with the same number and type of lamps.
- **Ballast Factor (BF)** = the light output of a commercial ballast / the light output of a reference

ballast. BF is a measure of the light output of an integrated lamp and ballast combination. The lower the BF the more efficient the system.

- **BTU** - One BTU equals the amount of energy required to raise the temperature of one pound of water by 1°F at sea level.
- **British Thermal Unit per Hour** – (BTUH) Cooling and Heating capacity measured per hour.
- **Bulb size** – the maximum diameter of a bulb expressed in eighths of an inch. (i.e. a T-8 fluorescent tube has a one-inch diameter).
- **Candela (cd)** – a measure of luminous intensity in a given direction.
- **Cogeneration** – is the term describing a unit that generates and utilizes both electricity and heat at the same time.
- **Color Rendering Index (CRI)** – on a scale of (1-100), a measure of how accurately a light source renders colors. Higher numbers describe truer colors. A CRI of 100 has no color distortion.
- **Compact Fluorescent Lamps (CFL)** – are lower wattage replacement lamps that now are available in sizes to retrofit nearly all standard usage incandescent lamps. They produce the same light levels while consuming up to 85% less energy and lasting at least ten times longer.
- **Conduction** – The process by which heat transfers along or through a substance (i.e. electric blanket).
- **Convection** - The process of transferring heat by movement of a gas (i.e. air) or a fluid.
- **Correlated Color Temperature (CCT)** – a measure of how warm (yellow to red) or cool (green to blue) a light appears (e.g. Warm is below 3000 K, cool is

above 5000K.). Astronomers use the same scale to describe star color.

- **Cost of light replacement formula** approximately 88% = cost of electricity; 8% = labor cost; 4% = cost of lamps.
- **Cubic Feet per Minute (CFM)** – a measurement of the movement of air within a space.
- **Current** - is the flow of electrons and is measured in Amperes. (I)
- **Daylight harvesting** – building design that takes advantage of outdoor lighting to reduce electrical usage.
- **Demand** – (On your electric bill) is the total value of power over a specified interval of time.
- **Diffuser** – spreads conditioned air from the end of an air duct into a space.
- **Driver** – an electrical device that works much like a ballast to provide the correct voltage to activate an LED light.
- **Direct Digital Controller** – a control system capable of controlling VAV (Variable Air Volume).
- **Economizer** – an A/C device that controls damper blade positions to regulate the outside air flowing into a system. It saves energy by bringing in 100% fresh air to replace the exhausted air when the condition of the exterior air (both temperature and humidity) closely approximates the interior air.
- **ECM (Electronically Commutated Motor)** – An extremely efficient brushless, permanent-magnet DC motor that has a money-saving application in both HVAC and refrigeration.

- **Efficacy** – The efficiency of a light source measured in lumens/watt.
- **Electric Motor Efficiency** - the useable horsepower that is obtained as a percent of the power that goes into a motor.
- **Electroluminescence** – the process of directly converting electrical energy into visible light, which is the basis for LED technology.
- **EIS (Energy Information Systems)** – is a communication tool that meshes together input from internal systems with external data like weather, electricity prices and real-time power consumption.
- **EMI (Electromagnetic Inference)** – high frequency radio waves are generated by some electronic ballasts that can interfere with radio and TV transmission. This becomes critical in stores using radio frequency driven equipment.
- **EMS system** – A computer-based device that controls HVAC, lighting and other building systems.
- **Energy Efficiency Ratio (EER)** - is a measurement of A/C cooling capacity in systems with greater than 65,000 BTU/hr (5.4 tons). The current California minimum EER Rating is 11.5.
- **Enhanced Automation** – is an umbrella term that includes BAS (Building Automation Systems), EMS (Energy Management Systems) and EIS (Energy Information Systems). BAS and EMS are essentially the same. (See EMS.) Some of the controllable elements include: thermostat settings, supply air, occupancy controls, demand control ventilation, lighting controls and ASD fans.
- **Evaporative Coolers** – AKA "swamp coolers" pull warm, dry exterior air through moist pads to condition

the air, then blow the newly cooled air into a space with a simple fan.

- **Floodlight** – is a luminaire/lamp that disperses a bright light in a beam over 20° wide. (See also Spotlight.)
- **Fluorescent Lamp** – a high efficiency lamp that sparks an electric discharge through a mixture of inert gas and mercury vapor to produce ultraviolet (UV) energy. Phosphors on the interior lamp surface convert the energy to light.
- **Footcandle (FC)** – Measure of incident light. One footcandle is the amount of light generated by one candle hitting a surface from one foot away.
- **Frequency** – the rate of alternation of AC current expressed in Hertz (Hz).
- **Fuel Cells** – is a galvanic cell or "battery" that continuously converts chemical energy to electrical energy and heat without combustion. It is two or three times as efficient as an internal combustion engine and never needs to be recharged.
- **Heat Pumps** – move heat from a source location to a heat sink location. While cooling, the heat pump moves hot air from inside to outside. While heating, the refrigerant cycle reverses to remove heat from outside and send it inside.
- **HEPA (High Efficiency Particle Absorption)** is a measure of the effectiveness of air filters.
- **High-Bay lighting** – lighting designed typically for industrial use in ceilings at 20' or more.
- **High Intensity Discharge Lamps (HID)** – produce light with an electric arc in a small tube within the body of the lamp.

- **High Power Factor** – is accomplished in a ballast by using a capacitor to increase its efficiency to over 90%.
- **High Pressure Sodium** – emit a golden color that still distorts colors but not as much as low pressure sodium. They are best in applications where color is not critical to task performance (i.e. a warehouse).
- **Hot Restart Time** – the time it takes an HID lamp to reach a 90% light output after being turned off, then on.
- **Incandescent Lamp** – invented by Thomas Edison, is a generally inefficient light source that drives electricity through a very thin (usually tungsten) wire causing it to glow white-hot.
- **Indirect Lighting** – points luminaries toward the ceiling which produces a softer, more diffused light scattered over a wider area.
- **Induction Lamps** – are essentially electrodeless fluorescents lamps with an anticipated useful life of 100,000 hours.
- **Instant Start Lamps** – are ignited by high voltage without preheating the filament.
- **Integral** – is a term used to describe the built-in ballast or drive in a Compact Fluorescent Lamp (CFL).
- **Kilowatt (kW)** = volts x amps / 1000.
- **Kilowatt Hour (kWh)** – the standard billing unit used by utilities for electrical usage. (i.e. Ten 100 watt lamps burning for one hour consumes one kilowatt hour of electricity.)
- **Lamp** – Consumers refer to an incandescent light as a light bulb and a fluorescent light as a tube. The lighting industry calls them both lamps.

- **LED** – Light emitting diode.
- **Light** – radiant energy that can be seen by the human eye.
- **Light Pollution** – light directed to where it is unneeded. The most common light pollution is directed skyward which hides starlight.
- **Light Trespass (spillage)** – misdirected light that is disturbing, irritating and/or potentially dangerous.
- **Load Shedding** – reducing lighting or other electrical usage in response to a need in support of the grid.
- **Low Pressure Sodium Lamps** – Introduced in 1932, are the most efficient lighting source with the longest life. However, their monochromatic yellow color restricts their usage to street lamps and outdoor parking or storage areas where distinguishing color is not important.
- **Lumen** – a measure of quantity of light emitted by a source.
- **Luminaire** – a lighting industry term for the fixture that encompasses the entire lighting system.
- **Luminous Efficacy** – is a measure of lamp brightness measured in lumens per watt. The higher the lumens per watt, the more light you are getting for the amount of electricity you are using.
- **Make-up Air (Outside Air)** – Air brought in from outside to replace air that has been removed by exhaust fans.
- **Mercury Vapor Lamps** – are the oldest type of HID lamp. Because of the huge energy savings, they are being systematically replaced by newer metal halide lamps or high pressure sodium lamps.

- **MERV (Minimum Efficiency Reporting Value)** – a rating for air filter efficiency. Air filters with a MERV rating over 8 are recommended for Supermarkets.
- **Metal Halide Lamps** – the newer generation lamps are available in two main types. 1) Pulse-start metal halides which use about 20% less energy than the traditional metal halides and 2) Ceramic Metal Halides (CMH) which are used where high quality, directional light is needed.
- **Microturbines** – are small, (under 500 kW) highly efficient combustion turbines that can run on a variety of fuels and can fit in small spaces. They are used to generate electricity, heat or cooling.
- **MR-16** – a common 2" diameter mirrored reflector halogen or ceramic metal halide lamp.
- **Occupancy Sensors** – A device that activates lighting after sensing the presence of a person to switch lighting on only when a room is occupied. There are four main types: Passive Infrared, Ultrasonic, Microphonic, and Hybrid.
- **Operating or Burn Position** – Certain lamps are made to burn in specific orientations (i.e. facing up or down). The wrong orientation shortens the rated life of the lamp and may create safety issues.
- **PCB (Polychlorinated Biphenyls)** – A class of organic compounds used in old style ballasts. It is extremely hazardous to the environment because it is cumulative and does not break down in nature.
- **Photo Detector (Photometer)** – A device that measures light often used in daylight harvesting situations.
- **Photometrics** – is the measure of the intensity of light measured at specified angles around the fixture.

- **Photovoltaics** – unlike solar power technologies, a photovoltaic system converts light directly into electricity using a chemical reaction in semiconductor materials.
- **Power (P)** - is measured in horsepower or watts. (W)
- **Programmable Thermostat** – gives you the option of setting different room temperatures based on time of day and day of the week.
- **Programmed Rapid Start** – a lamp starting method that preheats the lamp filaments before ignition. This type of lamp/ballast combination has a longer life.
- **Radiation** – As it relates to temperature, radiation is the use of energy waves to change the temperature of solid objects (i.e. sunlight).
- **Rated Lamp Life** - the number of hours 50% of a test sample of lamps burned before burning out.
- **Relative Humidity** – the measure of how much moisture the air is holding as a percentage of how much it could hold.
- **Relief Air** - Air exhausted outside to allow fresh make-up air to enter the space.
- **Resistance (R)** - is the property of a conductor that restricts electric current flow.
- **Return Air** – Untreated air that is returning to the A/C unit from the space.
- **ROI** – (Return on Investment) – typically noted as a percentage or as a function of time.
- **Seasonal Energy Efficiency Ratio (SEER)** - applies to both commercial and residential systems with capacities less than 65,000 BTU/hr (5.4 tons). The minimum SEER rating in the United States is 13. The maximum is 21.

- **Self-ballasted Lamps** – a discharge lamp (e.g. HIDs or CFLs) that has a ballast incorporated into the lamp allowing for direct connection.
- **Sick Building Syndrome** – is the result of, among many things, poor ventilation, carbon dioxide build-up, mold, ineffective lighting and generally poor design. It is particularly prevalent in older buildings.
- **Spot Light** – a reflector lamp with a tight beam of light, typically around 10°. (See also Flood lamp.)
- **Supply Air** – Air that is leaving the A/C unit and being introduced into the space.
- **Sustainability** – is a philosophy that seeks to find ways to reduce or eliminate the negative impact of buildings on the environment and its occupants.
- **T-5** – a 5/8" diameter fluorescent tube created in Europe on a metric scale. They are more efficient than both T-8's and T-12's but are not a viable retrofit option because of their shorter length and optimum compatibility with high frequency electronic ballasts.
- **T-8** – a 1" diameter (8/8") fluorescent tube. They burn about 23% less electricity than a T-12 while producing the same light levels.
- **T-12** – a 1.5" diameter (12/8") fluorescent tube. They are available in a variety of lengths and are the least efficient of the typically used fluorescent lamps.
- **Task lighting** – is the lighting used by workers to perform a particular task that requires more light than is provided by the ambient light source.
- **Ton of cooling** - one ton equals the amount of heat required to melt one ton of ice in 24 hours or 12,000 BTU per hour. Note: a one-ton cube of ice measures 5.6' on each side.

- **Transients** – High voltage surges that can be caused by electrical events ranging from lightning strikes to in-store short circuits.
- **Troffer** – a long, recessed lighting unit typically installed in a T-bar ceiling.
- **Up Lighting** – accent lighting and/or wall-wash lighting shining up toward the ceiling.
- **Valance Lighting** – above-eye-level wall lighting typically shielded by horizontal panels.
- **Volt** – a measure of the electrical potential between two points.
- **Voltage -** is the electrical pressure that causes current to flow. The unit of measure is volts. (E)
- **Watts** – a unit of electrical power indicating the rate at which electricity is consumed.

APPENDIX C

FACTS

GENERAL

- The number one best way to save energy is to TURN IT OFF!
- Sustainability isn't an all or nothing proposition. The building owner/operator can choose how far to go and how much to spend.
- If you design for human health/comfort, you will be designing for efficiency – but not the other way around.
- No building should ever be designed or maintained that significantly sacrifices personal comfort to save energy.
- Henry Ford first created the definition of horsepower. One horsepower is the work required to lift 550 lb. one foot in one second.
- The medical profession is using colored light to treat a wide range of disorders including depression, migraines, ulcers, arthritis, high blood pressure and anxiety.
- Fuses were created by the Fire Captains of America first, to save fireman's lives and secondly to save buildings.
- Energy efficient equipment produces more work for the same amount of current.
- Most energy is lost in the form of heat.

- Three phase systems are more efficient than one phase systems because they are easier to balance, reduce line loss, and create better motor operation.
- A single watt is equal in both AC and DC and in single or three phase conditions.
- Generators and motors operate essentially the same but opposite. Generators convert mechanical energy to electrical energy. Motors convert electrical energy to mechanical energy.

CONDITIONED AIR

- The typically preferred Relative Humidity range is 40 – 60%.
- The optimum air motion in an occupied space is 15 to 25 feet per minute.
- One person generates a 450 BTU/hour total heat gain. (latent + sensible)
- A one horsepower motor generates a 2,545 BTU/hour heat gain.
- A recent study showed that after only 18 months, only 10% of the test study thermostats were calibrated correctly.
- Typical office equipment generates .85 to 8.5 BTU/hour per square foot.
- Depending on your kitchen area, the airflow around kitchen exhaust hoods should be about 2500 CFM.
- Rigid, round air ducts are the most efficient.
- Three thousand watts of light generates 3400 BTUs.

LIGHTING AND ELECTRICITY

- User satisfaction increases when an occupant has control over the level of lighting in their workspace. Most people lower the lights below the design level and save energy by accident.
- One single 100-watt light bulb burning 18 hours a day for a year costs $100. Simply put, 100 watts cost $100/ year.
- Replacing one 100-watt incandescent screw-in lamp with a 23 watt CFL can save $77/ year.
- Using low temp CFLs in walk-in freezers saves up to $50/lamp.
- Replacing only four of the 75 or 100-watt incandescent lamps in your exhaust hoods can save up to $100/year.
- The first LED light was created during the 1920's. Their popularity soared in the 1990's when white and blue LED technology became more affordable.
- LED lighting does best in cold conditions. As temperatures rise, light output, efficacy, anticipated useful life and color quality all decrease.
- Replacing the lamps in your emergency exit signs with LEDs can save you $50/ sign each year.
- LED lights are more environmentally friendly than many other types of lamps because they contain no Mercury.
- LED estimated useful life figures are approximations since the technology is evolving so quickly.

- One footcandle of light is bright enough to see in a dim room. You need three footcandles of light to move around safely and twenty to thirty to read a newspaper.
- A recent study showed that 90% of the population would not notice a 10% in-store light reduction.
- Incandescent and fluorescent lamps lose 20 to 30% of their light output over their service life.
- Incandescent light bulbs are the least efficient light source because they convert about 90% of the energy used to heat. Another negative is their relatively short lamp life.
- Fluorescent lamps are more efficient than incandescent lamps because they convert a smaller proportion of the energy to heat and more to light.
- Most lamps must now be disposed of as hazardous waste.
- Lamp disposal is legally the generators' responsibility (i.e. the owner, not the installer).
- Metal Halide lamps are fast-starting/restriking, have a high CRI and good color rendering.
- Blue – green spectrum light is the most healthful because it enhances, not suppresses, serotonin production that affects cancer probability.
- Quartz Halogen lamps work essentially the same as regular incandescent lamps except they are filled with Halogen. These lamps reduce energy consumption by 25 to 50% and have an anticipated useful life of about 30,000 hours that more than offsets the higher initial cost.
- Programmed Start Ballasts are preferred in combination with occupancy sensors because they ensure optimum lamp life.

- Replacing T-12 lamps and their magnetic ballasts with T-8 lamps and electronic ballasts typically saves 30%.
- Occupancy sensors typically have a less than one-year payback.
- Background lighting should not be less than 1/3 to 1/2 of the required task lighting.
- Lamp diameters are measured in 1/8-inch increments. Therefore a T-12 has a 1.5" diameter and a T-5 has a 5/8" diameter. This system is also used to measure and describe a bulb-shaped lamp.

APPENDIX D

ON-LINE RESOURCES

Awarenessideas.com – Has the widest selection of energy-saving programs that we were able to find anywhere in the country. If they don't have exactly what you envision among their hundreds of thousands of items, they can help you design a custom program that exactly fits your needs. www.awarenessideas.com

Better Bricks – A Portland, Oregon-based resource dedicated to helping your company or store reap the bottom line benefits of intelligent energy management. A good source of ideas from store design to operations on how to reduce your energy consumption. www.betterbricks.com/subHomepage

BOMA – Building Owners and Managers Association – One of the nations leading resources to help building owners and managers wade through the sea of "green wash" to identify the best solutions to save money and energy. www.boma.org

CTAC – Consumer Technology Application Center – In Southern California, CTAC is the best source of in-depth information about all aspects of saving energy. Operated by SCE, their programs include: seminars, workshops, displays, demonstrations, technical consultations and facility presentations. www.sce/ctac.com

Davetroesh.com – This is the first book of several dealing with easy inexpensive ways to save money and energy. Other books will address drug stores, convenience stores, dollar stores, schools and churches. See www.davetroesh.com for more information.

EERE – Office of Energy Efficiency and Renewable Energy – Working in both the private and public sectors, the EERE coordinates all the nation's efforts to create clean, reliable and affordable energy technologies. The EERE is an excellent resource to learn about the best of the new products coming to market. www.eere.energy.gov

Energy Information Administration – Official U.S. Government Energy Statistics. One of the best sources of extremely in-depth information about energy related trends, supplies, forecasts and analysis. www.eia.doe.gov

Energy Star® – A joint program of the U.S. Environmental Protection Agency and the U.S. Department of Energy dedicated to helping both businesses and homeowners save money and protect the environment through energy-efficient products and practices. www.energystar.gov

Energy Star® Portfolio Manager – The Energy Star® Portfolio Manager is a free on-line tool that allows you to track, monitor and assess energy and water consumption and costs in your store. www.energystar.gov/benchmark

Food Marketing Institute – A great resource for all things food-related including public affairs, safety, research, education, industry and government relations. www.fmi.org

Food Services Technology Center – the industry leader for testing appliance performance and commercial kitchen energy efficiency. Besides being a clearinghouse of information on equipment performance, the FSTC also has expertise in commercial kitchen ventilation and building energy efficiency, including lighting, glazing and HVAC. www.fishnick.com

Lamp recycling – All fluorescent lamps (including CFLs) contain mercury, which is classified as a hazardous material. Lamprecycle.org is a one stop information source for how to recycle your old lamps in the US and Canada. www.lamprecycle.org

APPENDIX E

SAMPLE
VENDOR PREVENTATIVE MAINTENANCE CHECKLIST

REFRIGERANT LEAK CHECK (Refrigeration)

- o Repair all accessible refrigeration leaks as part of this PM.
- o Inspect machine room piping.
- o Inspect machine room compressor racks.
- o Inspect pressure relief valve or vent outlets.
- o Inspect heat reclaim coil and associated valves.
- o Inspect roof equipment.
- o Inspect overhead piping, including warehouse and catwalks.
- o Inspect walk-in cooler and freezer coils.
- o Inspect all refrigerated cases and underground riser feeds.

REFRIGERANT LEAK CHECK (HVAC)

- o Repair all refrigerant leaks as part of this PM.
- o Inspect A/C compressors and related components.
- o Inspect cooling coil and related piping.
- o Inspect condenser, both while it is running at its fullest and while all the related compressor equipment is shut down.

GENERAL MAINTENANCE (Refrigeration)

- o Examine compressor systems for potential piping or electrical rubouts (silicone as needed).

- Inspect systems for loose cap tubes or hoses (silicone as needed).
- Inspect all case connections, honeycombs, reach-in door hinges, and gaskets. Repair as needed.
- Inspect contactors for pitting and wear (replace as needed).
- Test all oil failure controls.
- Test demand control modules.
- Inspect and clean compressor body cooling fan blades and mounts (tighten bolts as needed).
- Verify that high-pressure controls are not set above 300lbs. for R22 and 375lbs. for 404a.
- Verify proper oil level in compressors.
- List compressor superheats.

  ____

  ____
- Remove all trash from machine room.

CONDENSERS (AIR COOLED AND EVAPORATIVE)

- Inspect shaft and bearings and LUBE.
- Inspect belts – Replace and adjust as needed. (DO NOT OVERTIGHTEN)
- Inspect all motors. Verify they are operational.
- Inspect evaporative condensers for calcium buildup.
- Confirm pumps and sprayers are operational on evaporative condensers.
- Check and clean air-cooled condensers as required by ambient conditions.
- Evaporative condenser last date of service: ________

EMS

- Calibrate float sensors for rack float.
- Calibrate suction, discharge and drain line transducers.

- Confirm that all Variable Speed Drives are on line and not in bypass.
- Confirm all racks are floating.

HVAC

- Exercise A/C compressor and verify unloader valve setting.
- Inspect direct drive compressors for coupling damage.
- Verify that store does not have negative pressure.
- Confirm rooftop exhaust and make-up air units are working.
- Inspect all rooftop units for bearing wear and worn belts or pulleys.
- Lubricate all motors.
- Replace all air filters as scheduled.
- Replace worn belts. (DO NOT OVERTIGHTEN BELTS.)
- Inspect condenser motors and replace as needed.
- Verify condition of contactors and motor starters for pitting. Replace as needed.
- Check pressure drops across suction filters.
- Check pressure drops across driers.
- Perform no condensable test.
- Perform acid test.
- Check wire tightness.
- Inspect ductwork for leaks and blockage, especially the 90° turns.

GENERAL

- Clean all walk-in cooler and freezer coils as needed.
- Clean all self-contained condensers.
- Remove old parts, compressors, used oil, refrigeration cylinders from store.
- Below list all open issues to discuss with management.

APPENDIX F

The "ENERGY SURVEY FOR EMPLOYEES" below is downloadable from www.awarenessideas.com. While you are on their website, take a look at all the other energy related ideas to help promote your sustainability program.

Ask your associates to take this survey now, and in six months, ask them to take it again. It will be a good measure of the effectiveness of your environmental message.

Energy Survey For Employees

Thank you for taking the time to fill out this Energy Awareness Questionnaire. Put an X in the column under each question describing your opinions on each question. We will use your opinions to help shape our energy awareness plans, help save energy and promote our energy conservation efforts. Your time and effort is appreciated!

	None	Low/NO	So-So	Good/YES	Excellent
How would you rate our companies top management's commitment to energy conservation?					
Do you know the energy conservation goals of our company?					
Are the company's energy goals very well articulated?					
What is the consistency of energy messages from management?					
What is the level of visible attempts to communicate energy messages?					
Does the level of energy communications demonstrate strong management support?					
Do the energy messages being used have impact?					
Do energy messages get changed often?					
Is more emphasis on energy conservation than needed?					
Are energy saving projects given much employee awareness?					
Are successful energy projects given much acknowledgement?					
Does management offer opportunities to participate in energy reduction products?					
Are energy projects in process recognizable?					
Do you volunteer to participate in energy projects?					
Would you like to volunteer to participate in energy projects?					
Would more emphasis on energy conservation be meaningful to you?					
Would more emphasis on energy conservation be good for the company?					
Would you like to see more visible reminders of where to look for energy waste?					
Have you noticed much increase in energy conservation activities?					

Please hand this survey in to your supervisor as soon as possible. Thank you!

- Management

NOTES

Made in the USA
Monee, IL
04 November 2026

67385480R00056